The Child of Christmas

By Mark Potter

Illustrated by Gina Jackson

This book is given to ________________________

With love from ________________________

Merry Christmas!

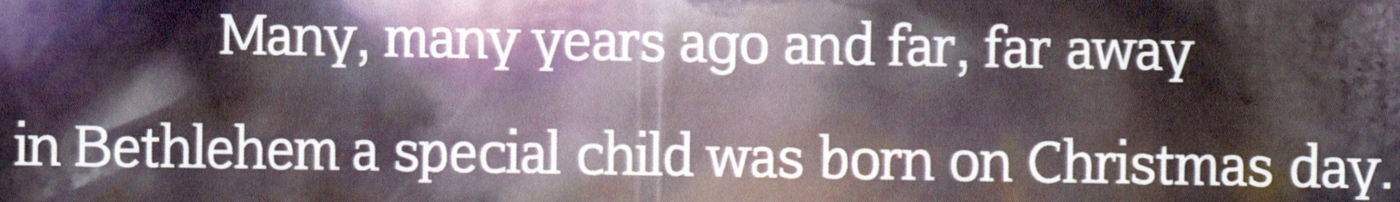

Many, many years ago and far, far away
in Bethlehem a special child was born on Christmas day.

This baby boy was wrapped in cloths,
and a manger's where he laid.
For in the inn there was no room; inside he could not stay.

"Glory to God and peace on earth!" the angels, they proclaimed.

Shepherds so longed to see this child

that they did not delay,

while wise men came from distant lands

to give Him gifts of praise.

You ask,

"Who is this child?"

"Who is this child?"

"What child is this?"

In Genesis, we see that...

He takes part in God's creation.

He's the ark of our salvation.

He's the covenant of grace.

He redeems the human race.

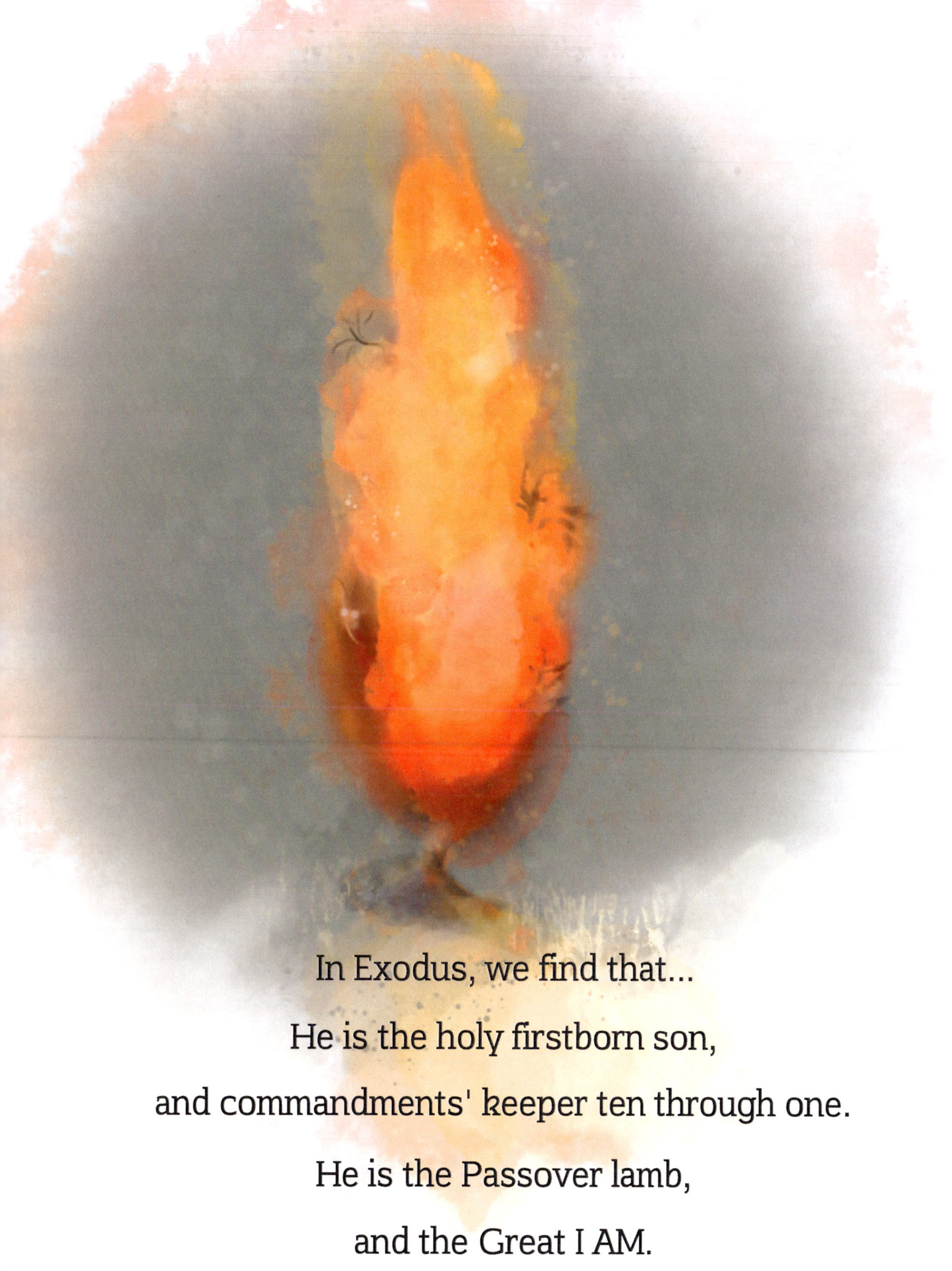

In Exodus, we find that...

He is the holy firstborn son,

and commandments' keeper ten through one.

He is the Passover lamb,

and the Great I AM.

You ask,
"Who is this child?"
"Who is this child?"
"What child is this?"

In Leviticus…

He is the tabernacle

and the great High Priest.

He is the scapegoat and sin offering

on the Day of Atonement feast.

In Numbers...
He's our shining star and sovereign scepter.
He's the water that quenches our thirst,
and the One through whom our curse would be
reversed.

You ask,
"Who is this child?"
"Who is this child?"
"What child is this?"

In Deuteronomy...
He is our inheritance
and our rock.
In Joshua...
He is our victory and
our deliverer.

In Judges...
He is our just Judge.
And in Ruth...
He is our kinsman Redeemer.

In Samuel...

He is the Lord of hosts.

In Kings...

He is the true prophet, priest, and king.

And in Chronicles...

He is our true Temple.

In Ezra...
He rebuilds and restores.
In Nehemiah...
He renews and unites.
In Esther...
He advocates and protects.
And in Job...
He endures and rewards.

You ask,

"Who is this child?"

"Who is this child?"

"What child is this?"

In Psalms...

He worships and shepherds.

In Proverbs...

He offers wisdom and direction.

In Ecclesiastes...

He brings meaning and hope.

In Song of Solomon...

We are His affection.

In Isaiah...
He is the suffering servant.
For by His stripes, we are healed.
He is wonderful Counselor,
Mighty God, everlasting Father,
And Prince of Peace.
In Jeremiah...
He is the righteous Branch,
And Israel's restorer.
In Lamentations...
He carries our grief.

In Ezekiel...
He is our watchman.
In Daniel...
He protects us in the fire.

In Hosea...
He forgives our impure ways.
In Joel...
He pours out his Spirit in these last days.

In Amos...

He fights for the oppressed.

In Obadiah...

He is the hope of Israel.

In Jonah...

He is God's missionary

who was buried in the belly of a whale.

In Micah...
He does justice,
loves mercy,
and walks humbly.

In Nahum...

He is our strength and shield.

In Habakkuk...

He is our prayerful intercessor.

In Zephaniah...

He is our warrior, Savior.

In Haggai...

He is our encourager.

In Zechariah...

He is Zion's King and coming Messiah.

In Malachi...

He is the refiner's fire.

You ask,

"Who is this child?"

"Who is this child?"

"What child is this?"

When we turn from the Old Testament to the New,
we learn that this child is the Holy and Righteous One,
God's only begotten Son.

He is the stone the builders rejected,

in whom we are protected,

and our faith is perfected.

He is the King of the Jews,

whose witness is forever faithful and true.

He is the resurrection and the life

and the bridegroom to our wife.

He is the church's head,

Heaven's bread,

and Judge of both the living and dead.

He is the chief cornerstone,

who hears creation groan.

He is the first and the last

who brings hope to generations

future, present, and past.

He is the firstborn over creation

and the horn of our salvation.

He is the Good Shepherd
and the gate for His sheep.
He is our provider,
whose harvest we will reap.

He is the heir of all things,
Lord of lords and King of kings.

He is God's holy Lamb,
Son of David, and Son of man.

Creator,
Deliverer,
Redeemer,
and Savior.

He is the world's Light.

He helps the blind receive sight.

He is the righteous and living one

for by his blood, sin's payment is done.

He's the Morning Star,

Mediator, Messiah,

and Master.

He's the person we pray to

in times of disaster.

He is earth's sovereign ruler
and God's infinite power,
yet He laid down His life
in His final hour.

He is the Lion of Judah
and the hope of glory.
He is the one in whom
we find our story.

He is the Great Physician
and the Word made flesh.

He is the last Adam
whose lordship we profess.

He is the life

and the truth

and the way.

He took on our debt,

which we could never repay.

He is the true vine who forgives sins, yours and mine.

He is Immanuel,
God with us,
setting free all those
who are treated unjust.

He is the Amen
and the final sacrifice for sin.

He is the Alpha,

the Omega,

the Beginning,

and...

...the End!

You ask,

"Who is this child?"

"Who is this child?"

"What child is this?"

This child,
this child
is Christ the King,
the one we call...

Jesus!

About the Author

Mark Potter is a devoted pastor, husband, and father of four boys. When Mark was suddenly diagnosed with cancer in July of 2020, he made a goal to write a book that he could read and discuss with each of his kids, no matter their age. His prayer is for each of them to know, love, and worship the Biblical Jesus. He dedicates this book to them, and to his beautiful, loving, and supportive wife, Emily.

About the Illustrator

Gina Jackson is a talented artist who brings beauty from her subconscious to life. Her honesty, mixed with years of study, imparts a unique quality to her illustrations. She works earnestly with thick layers to create rich textures, capturing the drama and elegance of everyday life. Her ultimate goal is to use her art to share the love and goodness of Jesus with as many people as possible.

www.ingramcontent.com/pod-product-compliance
Lightning Source LLC
Chambersburg PA
CBRC090145150726
48196CB00019B/734